**LARGE PRINT**

# READ ALOUD TALES of
# BRAVERY AND COURAGE

## Maharana Pratap
## and other stories...

Retold by
VANEETA VAID

Nita Mehta
Publications
Enriching Young Minds

# READ ALOUD TALES of
# BRAVERY AND
# COURAGE

## Maharana Pratap
## and other stories...

Nita Mehta
Publications
Enriching Young Minds

# LARGE PRINT
## READ ALOUD TALES of
# BRAVERY AND COURAGE
### Maharana Pratap
### and other stories...

Nita Mehta Publications

**Nita Mehta Publications**

Corporate Office
3A/3, Asaf Ali Road, New Delhi 110 002
Phone: +91 11 2325 2948, 2325 0091
Telefax: +91 11 2325 0091
E-mail: nitamehta@nitamehta.com
Website: www.nitamehta.com

ISBN 978-81-7676-135-2

First Print 2014

Printed in India at Infinity Advertising Services (P) Ltd, New Delhi

Distributed by :
NITA MEHTA BOOKS
3A/3, Asaf Ali Road, New Delhi - 02

Distribution Centre :
D16/1, Okhla Industrial Area, Phase-I,
New Delhi - 110020
Tel.: 26813199, 26813200
E-mail: nitamehta.mehta@gmail.com

Contributing Writers:
Subhash Mehta
Tanya Mehta

Editorial & Proofreading:
Rajesh
Ramesh

Editorial and Marketing office
E-159, Greater Kailash II, New Delhi 110 048

Typesetting by National Information Technology Academy
3A/3, Asaf Ali Road, New Delhi 110 002

Price: Rs. 145/-

# CONTENTS

# INTRODUCTION

Each era has its heroes. If ancient India saw Porus challenging the military might of Alexander, modern India showed Gandhi shaking the British imperialism by the power of his thoughts alone!

Through the pages of this book, we also learn about Razia Sultan, who emerged from behind her 'purdah' to take charge of her kingdom in difficult times.

These awe inspiring tales of bravery and courage will not only entertain but also inspire children.

# THE KING WHO COULD NOT BE DEFEATED

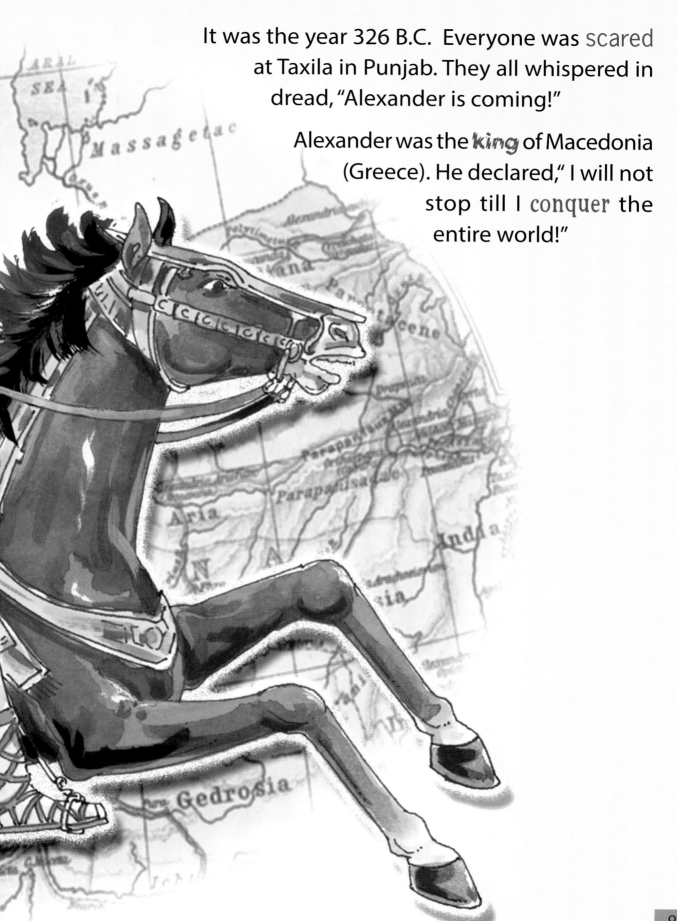

It was the year 326 B.C. Everyone was scared at Taxila in Punjab. They all whispered in dread, "Alexander is coming!"

Alexander was the king of Macedonia (Greece). He declared," I will not stop till I conquer the entire world!"

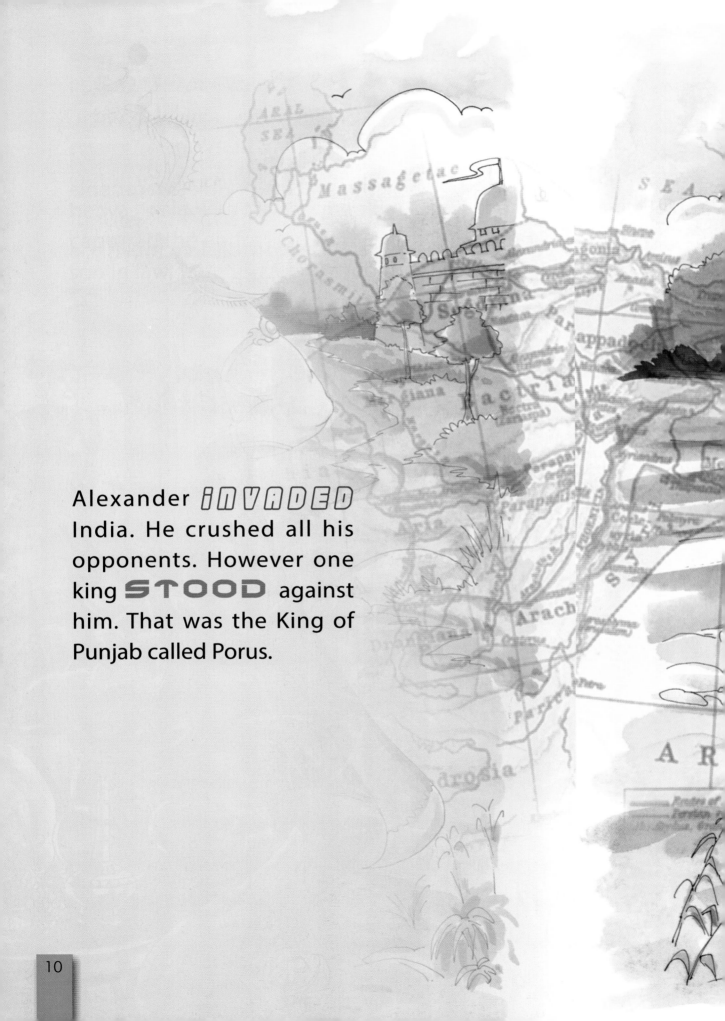

Alexander *INVADED* India. He crushed all his opponents. However one king **STOOD** against him. That was the King of Punjab called Porus.

Alexander angrily sent this message to Porus through a messenger, "Porus, come and meet me!"

Porus told the messenger, "I shall certainly meet him. Not in Taxila, but on the battle field."

Alexander accepted the challenge.

"Saddle Bucephalus,*" roared Alexander!

(*Bucephalus was Alexander's horse. Alexander rode through all his battles on this magnificent beast. Bucephalus died during the battle between Alexander and Porus. Alexander founded a city, Bucephala, in honour of the horse. The city lay on the west bank of the Hydaspes river (thought to be modern-day Jhelum in Pakistan).

A big battle between Porus and Alexander began.

Porus led a charge astride elephants. The battle field split with the neighs of the Macedonian horses and the trumpets of Porus's elephants. Dust and blood swirled. Unfortunately, Porus led a very heavy cavalry.

The elephants sunk deep into the muddy banks, making movement slower than usual. Alexander took advantage of this and surrounded Porus's army. From this moment on, the Indians were attacked from all sides. Eventually, nearly all of Porus's army was killed.

The wounded king Porus, surrendered only after the destruction of his entire army.

Chained & manacled, king Porus was presented before Alexander.

"Porus, you stand defeated before me. How would you like me to treat you now?" asked Alexander.

"Like a king," came Porus's proud answer, Alexander's expression changed to one of respect. He immediately ordered Porus's shackles to be removed.

"This brave king deserves to be released. His lands are to be returned to him." Thus, king Porus was released and his kingdom returned to him.

# RAZIA SULTAN

Qutub-ud-din Aibak was the first slave to rule Delhi. Before this, he was a slave to Muhammad Bin Ghori, the Muslim ruler, who captured the entire Northern India in 1192. In 1210 A.D. Aibak's son in law, Iltutmish succeeded the throne of Delhi.

When Iltutmish had to announce his successor, he said,

"My sons, Rukn-ud-din and Ghias-ud-din can think of only lavish life styles. I want to change my will. I want to name my daughter Razia as my successor after my death."

Shortly after this incident, the Sultan died. When it was announced that Razia, a woman, would be the successor, protests broke out. Seeing this, Razia told the noblemen, "I want to give the throne to Rukn-ud-din, my brother."

Sadly, he proved to be an irresponsible ruler. Not only did he ignore state duties, he spent all his time in drinking and enjoying himself. The noblemen wanted Razia back. Now Rukn-ud-din's mother was scared. She plotted to kill her step daughter, Razia. She wanted her son to remain as king!

The plot was uncovered by a foreign slave named Jamal-ud-din Yaqut. On the discovery of the plot, there was a revolt by the people. Razia was very popular with the masses.

Thus, Razia was crowned the ruler. She became the first woman ruler of the lands and was called 'Razia Sultan'.

Razia rewarded Yaqut, by making him the chief of all the noblemen! Razia was an efficient ruler. She donned the clothes of a man. She executed state matters competitively.

"Let my work speak for my actions," said Razia.

The noblemen however did not like her policies. Their hate increased when Razia abolished the Jaziah. This was a tax laid on non Muslims. The nobles objected to the appointment of Yaqut as their chief as well. Soon she was betrayed by her best friend Altunia. Altunia rebelled against Razia. Razia could not crush this revolt. Eventually, Yaqut was murdered and Razia captured to be imprisoned in Bhatinda.

Meanwhile in Delhi, Razia's half brother, Bahram Shah, was declared Sultan. In order to save her own life, Razia accepted Altunia's proposal of marriage. Once married, they marched to Delhi to reclaim the throne. However, before their army reached Delhi, Bahram's forces met them mid way and defeated their army. Razia and her husband were put to death on 14th October, 1240 A.D.

# THE BLIND ARCHER

Prithviraj Chauhan was the ruler of Delhi. Muhammad Ghori, the king of Ghor in Afghanistan, had grown very powerful.

The kingdom of Muhammad Ghori now stretched up to the domains of Prithviraj Chauhan, that is Delhi!

Muhammad Ghori first attacked the fort at Bhatinda. Prithviraj Chauhan was not prepared for this sudden attack! Hence, the army defending the city was defeated.

Prithviraj gathered an army to recapture the fort. The rival armies met at Tarain, near Thaneshwar. This time Prithviraj's army meted out a devastating defeat on Ghori's army. Muhammad Ghori himself was seriously injured and captured. Graciously, in a good will gesture, Prithviraj pardoned Ghori. Muhammad Ghori on his return to Ghazni, made frenzied plans for revenge.

The next year, Ghazni attacked again with an army of 1,20,000 men. Prithviraj collected an army too and faced Muhammad Ghori in Tarain.

But the circumstances were against Prithviraj. Ghori employed a strong reserve. Moreover, he did not get help from Jayachandra, the ruler of Gujarat.

Jayachandra hated Prithviraj Chauhan. Earlier Prithviraj Chauhan had eloped with Jayachandra's daughter.

Jayachandra had not forgiven Prithviraj for this. The battle was tough. Finally, Prithviraj was taken prisoner by Ghori's forces. As a prisoner in Ghor, Prithviraj was presented before Muhammad Ghori. Prithviraj Chauhan stood tall, looking at the Muslim king, straight into the eye.

Ghori felt insulted. He ordered Prithviraj to lower his eyes. A bold Prithiviraj refused! Enraged Ghori screamed, "Pierce these defiant eyes with sharp arrows!"

The terrible orders were carried out. Prithviraj was blinded.

One day, Ghori announced a contest of archery. What is archery? Archery is aiming at a target with a bow and arrow. Prithviraj heard of this contest. He asked to be included too.

Ghori teased him saying, "You are blind. You cannot participate in this contest!"

Prithviraj retorted, "I am confident of reaching my target. But on one condition."

"And what is that?" asked Ghori curiously.

"At the start of the game, you have to give me the order to shoot. I will only take orders from another King!"

Ghori agreed.

On the day of the game, Ghori ordered Prithviraj to shoot. Prithviraj, instead of aiming the arrow towards the target, aimed the arrow towards Ghori's voice. The arrow, with amazing accuracy, struck Muhammad Ghori and killed him. *

*There is no chronological confirmation to verify this story. Prithviraj was the last Hindu ruler of Delhi.

# MAHARANA PRATAP

Rana Pratap (1540-1597), was born in the kingdom of Mewar. In 1568, the Mughal emperor Akbar conquered Chittor, Mewar's capital. Rana Pratap was crowned King in 1572 at Mewar. He then began a life-long war against the Mughal Emperor Akbar to regain Mewar.

A famous battle was fought between Akbar and Rana Pratap. It is called the battle of Haldighati. Haldighati is a small village in the Aravalli Hills. On June 18, 1576, before sunrise, the two armies poised for attack at the Haldighati Pass.

Rana Pratap sat proudly upon Chetak, his handsome white Arab stallion. The horse wore coats resembling a grotesque elephant! The aim was to scare the enemy's horses.

The other reason for dressing the horse like an elephant was to mislead the elephants. It was assumed that elephants would not harm who they thought were small and young elephants.

On seeing Man Singh, a Rajput general with the Mughals, Rana Pratap was furious.

He charged towards Man Singh yelling, "You traitor!"

"Neighhhhhhh!" During this encounter, Chetak skidded to a halt in a cloud of dust. He abruptly collided with Man Singh's elephant's plate armour. Chetak was grievously wounded. Unaware of this, Rana Pratap continued fighting.

He killed the mahout (charioteer) riding Man Singh's elephant. Then, in the scuffle of bows and arrows, Man Singh disappeared!

Pratap let out a triumphant cry of revenge, "I have killed Man Singh!"

Startled by this cry, Man Singh's rider-less elephant ran in panic. Man Singh who had actually ducked on the side of his elephant had not been killed! "Hark!" He sprang back with a war cry. Steel rang against steel.

The battle raged for four hours. It seemed like the Mughals were in retreat. But then the Mughal reserves came into the battlefield.

By sun set, when the bugles announced the end of the day's battle, the Mughal reserves began to get an upper hand over Rana's forces. However, the Mewar **warriors** fought with raw courage, refusing to back off.  Rana Pratap sustained fatal wounds. If he died all would be lost. His horse Chetak came to his rescue.

A limping Chetak carried his master out of danger. But, after ensuring that his master was safe, the noble horse died.

Despite temporary victory for the Mughals, the battle of Haldighati is noteworthy for the persistence demonstrated by the Rajputs.*

---

* It is often remarked that the Rajputs of olden days treated war like a sport! For them, chivalry and correct code of conduct was like breathing.

# DANDI MARCH

One morning, in the early 1930's, at his ashram on the banks of the Sabarmati river, a very preoccupied Bapu, was spinning khadi on his personal spindle.

Who was Bapu? Bapu was Mohandas Karamchand Gandhi, also known as Mahatma Gandhi. He believed in non-violence and Satyagraha.

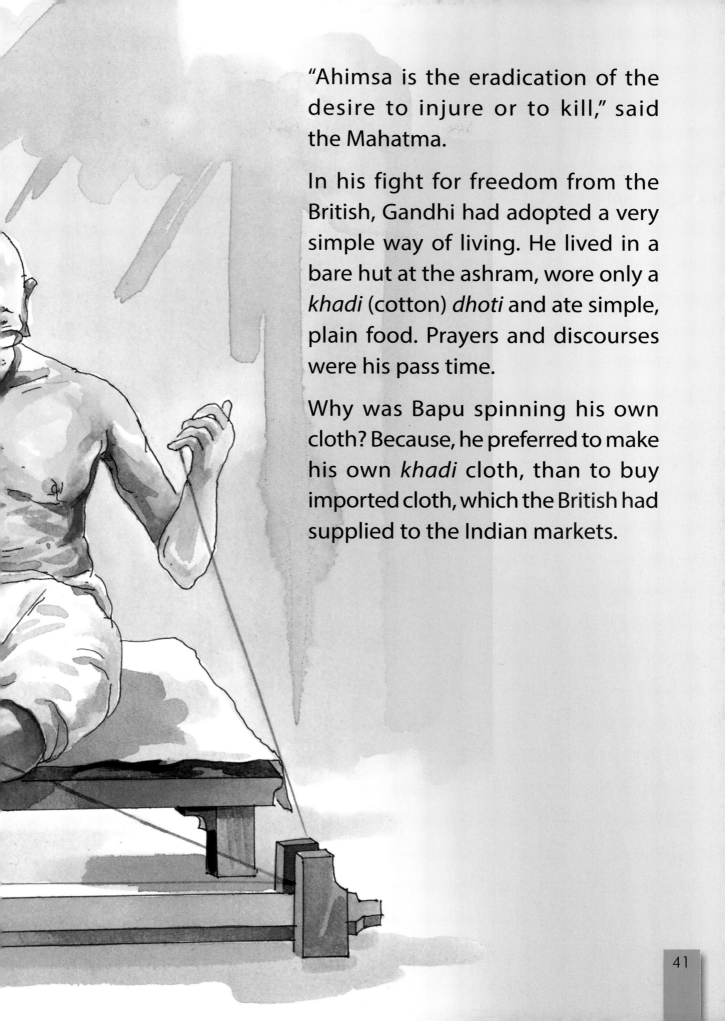

"Ahimsa is the eradication of the desire to injure or to kill," said the Mahatma.

In his fight for freedom from the British, Gandhi had adopted a very simple way of living. He lived in a bare hut at the ashram, wore only a *khadi* (cotton) *dhoti* and ate simple, plain food. Prayers and discourses were his pass time.

Why was Bapu spinning his own cloth? Because, he preferred to make his own *khadi* cloth, than to buy imported cloth, which the British had supplied to the Indian markets.

There was a tax on salt, in those days. Gandhi knew how important salt was for the common man. He wrote to the Viceroy very politely and explained why there should be no tax on salt, which was an essential commodity. Unfortunately, the Viceroy sent his regrets and did not abolish the salt tax. In protest, on 5th March, 1930, Gandhi announced to his followers, "We shall march to the seashore of Dandi and make our own salt."

That is why on March 12th, 1930, with seventy-eight of his followers and disciples from Sabarmati Ashram, Bapu set out on a 241 mile march to Dandi. With great confidence, Bapu marched ahead.

"Raghupati Raghava Raja Ram," Bapu's favorite hymn suddenly filled the air. All his followers sang together. The softly singing crowd, following Bapu, swelled. Finally, the long march ended on 5th April. On April 6th, the Mahatma picked up a lump of mud and salt and declared, "With this, I am shaking the foundation of the British Empire."

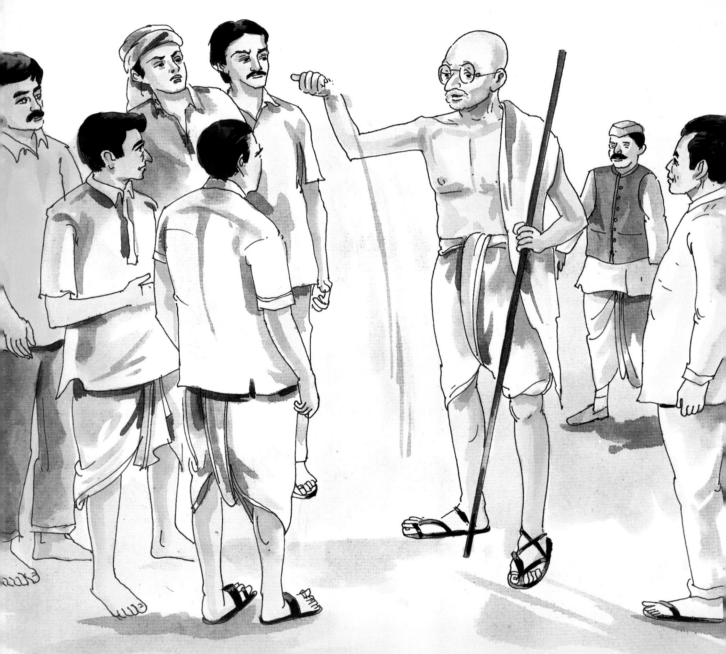

He then boiled the lump in seawater to make salt. By this act, Bapu had broken a law!

No sooner had Bapu broken the law, everywhere, others followed him. This created a panic in the British government.

"Arrest the rebels," they announced! Within one week, the jails were full.

Bapu was near Dandi when he was arrested.

The news of the Dandi March and Gandhi's arrest spread. The Dandi March brought into sharp focus the Indian freedom movement both in India as well as abroad.

After Gandhi's release from prison, he continued to work towards Indian independence, which was achieved on 15th August, 1947. There is no doubt that the Dandi March was a turning point in the freedom struggle.

The image of Gandhi, walking with firm steps, with a stick in hand, became symbolic and is a picture which inspires many even today.